ADVENT
in NARNIA

HEIDI HAVERKAMP

ADVENT *in* NARNIA

Reflections for the Season

WESTMINSTER
JOHN KNOX PRESS
LOUISVILLE · KENTUCKY

© 2015 Heidi Haverkamp

First edition
Published by Westminster John Knox Press
Louisville, Kentucky

15 16 17 18 19 20 21 22 23 24—10 9 8 7 6 5 4 3 2 1

Unless otherwise indicated, Scripture quotations are from the New Revised Standard Version of the Bible, copyright © 1989 by the Division of Christian Education of the National Council of the Churches of Christ in the U.S.A., and are used by permission. Scripture quotations marked CEB are from the Common English Bible, © 2011 Common English Bible, and are used by permission. Scripture quotations marked KJV are from the King James or Authorized version of the Bible.

Narnia is a trademark of C. S. Lewis (Pte.) Ltd. This book has not been prepared, endorsed, or licensed by any person or entity affiliated with C. S. Lewis (Pte.) Ltd. or related properties.

Book design by Drew Stevens
Cover design by designpointinc.com

Library of Congress Cataloging-in-Publication Data

Haverkamp, Heidi.
  Advent in Narnia : reflections for the season / Heidi Haverkamp. — First edition.
     pages cm
  ISBN 978-0-664-26126-9 (alk. paper)
  1. Lewis, C. S. (Clive Staples), 1898-1963. Lion, the witch, and the wardrobe. 2. Fantasy fiction, English—History and criticism. 3. Christian fiction, English—History and criticism. 4. Christianity in literature. 5. Narnia (Imaginary place) I. Title.
  PR6023.E926L4337 2015
  823'.912—dc23

                                                    201500275

PRINTED IN THE UNITED STATES OF AMERICA

♾ The paper used in this publication meets the minimum requirements of the American National Standard for Information Sciences—Permanence of Paper for Printed Library Materials, ANSI Z39.48-1992.

Most Westminster John Knox Press books are available at special quantity discounts when purchased in bulk by corporations, organizations, and special-interest groups. For more information, please e-mail SpecialSales@wjkbooks.com.

CONTENTS

INTRODUCTION

———— ⦿⦿ ————

*Do not deceive yourselves. If you think that you are wise in this age,
you should become fools so that you may become wise. For the wisdom
of this world is foolishness with God.* —1 Corinthians 3:18–19a

I read *The Lion, the Witch, and the Wardrobe* for the first time
when I was in elementary school. I loved to stare at the
cover, a picture of the four children in fur coats, framed
by a forest with the White Witch's castle looming behind
them. They looked like kids I might know. The lamppost
was like lampposts in my Chicago neighborhood, but it
stood by itself in the distance. The castle told me that this
was a fairy tale, which thrilled me. It was both familiar and
unfamiliar: a whole world on the other side of a closet door.

C. S. Lewis said that he began to write the Narnia
Chronicles because an image appeared in his mind: a faun
with an umbrella and his arms full of packages, walking
under a lamppost in the middle of a snowy forest. He also
saw a queen riding in a sleigh and a majestic lion. As he
wrote, "At first there wasn't anything Christian about
them; that element pushed itself in of its own accord."[1] The
novel unfolded as a work of imagination and faith.

When we deeply trust something we can't see, we must
use our imaginations. Consider Hebrews 11:1: "Now faith
is the assurance of things hoped for, the conviction of things

not seen." Too often, Christianity may seem to be a known quantity. We can take its radical values for granted and see Jesus as a cliché instead of our Savior. Lewis, by placing Christianity into another world, makes it unfamiliar again. He gives us the chance to feel a newfound wonder at the depth of God's love, the power of Christ's grace and the totality of his sacrifice, and the wonder of a world infused with the Holy Spirit. We all can use a spiritual wake-up call like this, whether we aren't sure Christianity can mean anything to us or whether it means everything.

Entering Narnia, though, means becoming a little bit "foolish," as St. Paul would put it. Reading children's literature might be embarrassing for adults or teenagers, but it can be a deep source of wisdom (and fun); as Lewis wrote, "When I was ten, I read fairy tales in secret and would have been ashamed if I had been found doing so. Now that I am fifty I read them openly."[2]

In 2013, I first thought to use *The Lion, the Witch, and the Wardrobe* for an adult Advent series at my church. We had a wonderful time reading the book; watching scenes from one of the movies; discussing spiritual imagination, temptation and repentance, lions and beavers, witches and fauns. It was such a rich experience that I wanted to share it with other individuals and churches as a way to observe Advent and prepare for Christmas.

Lewis's first book about the land of Narnia is a perfect fit for the season of Advent. The snow, a glowing lamppost, the children, the waiting for the return of a savior, and the visit of Father Christmas make it a natural reading partner for this time of year. The novel very quickly moves from Advent into Christmas, then Good Friday and finally to Easter; so, for the most part, the reflections and activities in this book focus on the first half of the novel, which is most pertinent to Advent.

There is a whole theological world Lewis created in the Narnia Chronicles (for more on this, read Rowan Williams's book *The Lion's World*), and while I do refer to *The Magician's Nephew* and *The Last Battle*, I focus on the characters, images, and themes of the first novel.

You can read along in *The Lion, the Witch, and the Wardrobe* as you do this Advent study; relevant chapters are listed at the start of the reflections that focus on the novel. Other devotions reflect primarily on Scripture or make only general reference to the novel. Reading the novel in its entirety is not necessary to understand or enjoy the reflections. You can watch one of the movie versions, if you'd prefer (see appendix A for details on the three most commonly available). Either strategy will help you get the most out of the reflections, the discussion sessions, and the "Narnia Night" for families.

However, my purpose in writing this book is not to help you to know Narnia better but to know God better. Rowan Williams wrote about Lewis, "The reader is brought to Narnia for a little in order to know Aslan better in this world."[3] I hope that by spending a little time in Narnia this Advent, you will get to know Aslan—and Jesus Christ—better, and to prepare for Jesus' birth at Christmas all the more richly for it.

—*Heidi Haverkamp*
Bolingbrook, Illinois

WEEK ONE

1. THROUGH THE WARDROBE

Strive to enter through the narrow door; for many, I tell you, will try to enter and will not be able. —*Luke 13:24*

To follow along in the novel, read chapter 1.

Four children, two sisters and two brothers, have been sent from their home in London to the countryside to escape the bombing of the Blitz during World War II. They're in a new place, living apart from their parents, with two adult caretakers who are mostly absent.

One rainy day, when they're exploring the big, lonely house where they're staying, Lucy, the youngest child, finds a large wardrobe all by itself in an empty room. She's curious; she opens the door and climbs in, pushing her way through the fur coats hanging inside, and then she's in the middle of a snowy forest.

When I was little, I would walk into closets with my arms in front of me, hoping to feel cold air and hear snow crunching under my feet. Maybe you did too. Something in me longed to find a world more like the one I wanted to believe in than the one that was around me.

Walking into Advent can be like walking through the wardrobe. Depending on where you live, Advent might even be like Narnia—cold, with snow under your feet. But Advent is like Narnia in more ways than weather. It's a magical time, set apart from ordinary time: we listen to special music; we decorate our homes, streets, and clothes; we eat particularly delightful and delicious foods. We experience a heightened sense of excitement and expectation. Those expectations are not only about the giving and receiving of gifts but also about Advent and Christmastime offering us a glimpse of a world that's kinder, more just, and more joyful than the one we usually experience.

To truly enter that world, as Christians, the door we must walk through first is Christ. Snow, greenery, music, cookies, and gifts can all help us imagine the kingdom of God, but no matter how big and beautiful the wreath, walking through our front door is not going to transform our lives the way walking through the door of Jesus himself will. It is he who will lead us to that world we long for, where pain is turned to love, and death to life.

Questions for Reflection

1. Which of your traditional Advent activities and preparations are most meaningful to you? Have you ever reflected on how they reveal something of Jesus to you? For instance, his love, grace, or care for the poor?
2. The image of Christ as "the narrow door" is sometimes viewed as an escape from the people we disagree with or as a way to make ourselves feel more special than others. How can that "door" be an invitation instead of a barrier?

2. THE LAMPPOST

The light shines in the darkness, and the darkness did not overcome it. —John 1:5

To follow along in the novel, read chapter 1.

We expect to see evergreen trees, snow, and glowing lights in Advent: outdoors, in stores, and on Christmas cards. Lucy Pevensie, however, is surprised to see a light glowing through snowy trees when she walks through the wardrobe. She's so curious about that light that she spends ten minutes walking to reach it.

A lamppost in a forest is a familiar image if you know the Narnia books, but it's meant to be surprising. Lewis leaves it unexplained in this novel, but in a later one, we learn that it grew from an earthly lamppost, which was used as a weapon by the White Witch then transformed into this lonely but shining light by Aslan (in *The Magician's Nephew*). Mr. Tumnus tells Lucy it's the boundary between Narnia and "the wild woods of the west." In the last chapter, the children come upon the lamppost and don't recognize it, but they notice how old it is and that it is dwarfed by the ancient trees around it.

This lamppost is a living thing. No one lights it, no one extinguishes it, and it burns without fuel. The White Witch's winter hasn't snuffed it out. It is a boundary, but also a promise that Aslan can make broken things new and alive. It is a beacon in the face of the dark, cold spell that lies on the land.

An Advent wreath and Christmas lights shine with the same kind of light. Jesus is the Light of the World, shining in a darkness of despair, sin, and death. A Light that, like the lamppost, was there in the beginning with God. A Light that was broken and made new in the Resurrection. A Light that shines through the darkness on all people. A Light that beckons us to be curious and to come and see.

Questions for Reflection

1. What special lights have you placed around your house this season, if any, to remind you of the "light coming into the world" (John 1:9)? If you haven't hung any lights, are there places you might like to, if you had the time or resources?

2. Anne Lamott writes, "Lighthouses don't go running all over an island looking for boats to save; they just stand there shining."[4] Does this also describe the Light of Christ? Why or why not?

3. What metaphor would you use to describe the light of Christ in your life this season? It might be glowing brightly, faintly, or off in the distance. Try writing a poem or prayer with that metaphor or with the metaphor of the lamppost.

3. A GREAT LIGHT

The people who walked in darkness
    have seen a great light;
those who lived in a land of deep darkness —
    on them light has shined.
. . . .
For the yoke of their burden,
    and the bar across their shoulders,
    the rod of their oppressor,
    you have broken as on the day of Midian.
For all the boots of the tramping warriors
    and all the garments rolled in blood
    shall be burned as fuel for the fire.
For a child has been born for us,
    a son given to us;
authority rests upon his shoulders;
    and he is named
Wonderful Counselor, Mighty God,
    Everlasting Father, Prince of Peace.
                    —Isaiah 9:2, 4–6

Every year after the Christmas Eve service I take a few leftover bulletins for planning next year's service. One year, I took one whose owner had made little notes in the margins. Next to the lines about warrior boots and "garments rolled in blood," the person had written "!!!!!!"

For centuries, Christian tradition has believed the coming of Jesus is foretold in this passage and read it at Christmastime. The language is beautiful, "The people walking in darkness," "A child has been born for us," "Wonderful Counselor, Mighty God, Eternal Father, Prince of Peace." But I wonder if we avert our eyes from those piles of burning boots and bloody clothes? Like the anonymous note-taker, perhaps we are shocked at first but quickly move on to the more familiar Christmas story.

Are blood and war really so out of place at Christmastime, or any time? War was looming for the Israelites and Judeans when Isaiah made his prophecy. The violence of Roman occupation was very real for the Jews of Jesus' time. Lucy must have walked into the wardrobe with the bombing and fires of the London Blitz still burning in her mind's eye. The creatures of Narnia live in the grip of a Witch who has frozen their land to ice and turns traitors to stone. We all walk with darkness or danger of some kind overshadowing our lives: warfare, cancer, poverty, broken relationships, depression.

God promises through Isaiah that, "On those living in a pitch-dark land, light has dawned." Aslan made a similar promise to Narnia in the light of a once-broken lamppost, and God promises the light of a burning fire as well, one that will destroy instruments of cruelty and suffering and guide our feet into the way of peace.

Questions for Reflection

1. What darkness looms in your life or your community right now? What "boots" or blood-stained clothes are you longing for God to destroy?
2. The holidays are a time when many people struggle with emotional darkness. If this is a difficult time of year for you, consider drawing or doodling a picture that depicts what that darkness feels like. Then draw or doodle a picture of the light you are longing for.

4. MR. TUMNUS

Go and learn what this means, "I desire mercy, not sacrifice." For I have come to call not the righteous but sinners. —Matthew 9:13

To follow along in the novel, read chapter 2.

Mr. Tumnus stumbles into Lucy at the lamppost with his arms full of wrapped packages. (Lucy wonders if he's been doing some Christmas shopping.) He drops all the packages into the snow in surprise when he sees a human girl in Narnia. Lucy doesn't drop any packages, but the faun is like no one she's seen before. He's half wild, with two goat legs, two horns, and a tail; and half tame, with a human upper body, red muffler, umbrella, and his tail folded over his arm.

Despite his kind greetings and docile appearance, Tumnus tries to kidnap Lucy. After serving her a meal of eggs and toast, he tries to sing her to sleep so that he can turn her over to the White Witch. He breaks down, confessing everything in tears but explaining he must betray her.

Lucy is just a little girl, but she's tougher than the faun and stands up for herself. While kindly offering her handkerchief for his copious tears, she insists he change his mind, that he *repent*. Her sense of justice and her kindness convert Tumnus; he changes his mind and chooses to become Lucy's friend instead of her kidnapper, even though it means putting himself in grave danger.

Advent is a season of repentance, and Mr. Tumnus is a good model for us. Like Tumnus, humans are wild and tame, fearful and loving, sinners and saints. Like Lucy, God calls us to account but also offers us love and mercy.

Questions for Reflection

1. Reflect on a time in your life when, feeling you were doing the right thing, you may actually have been acting in a way that hurt or betrayed someone else.
2. What would it mean to consider mistakes you've made, believing that God is both just and merciful? Does it make it easier to offer up your sins? Harder?
3. Which is harder for you: to confront others when they have hurt you or to be merciful to them? Why?

5. REPENTANCE

In those days John the Baptist appeared in the wilderness of Judea, proclaiming, "Repent, for the kingdom of heaven has come near." This is the one of whom the prophet Isaiah spoke when he said,
  "The voice of one crying out in the wilderness:
  'Prepare the way of the Lord,
    make his paths straight.'"
Now John wore clothing of camel's hair with a leather belt around his waist, and his food was locusts and wild honey. Then the people of Jerusalem and all Judea were going out to him, and all the region along the Jordan, and they were baptized by him in the river Jordan, confessing their sins. —Matthew 3:1–6

John the Baptist is also a hairy, wild man who lives on the border between two kingdoms. Tumnus meets Lucy at the border between Narnia and the wardrobe, and people come from all over Judea to meet John at the Jordan, where he stands at the border between what has been and the kingdom to come.

When they find him, out in the desert wilderness east of Jerusalem, it's to confess their sins and be baptized in the river. They are coming to prepare themselves for the coming of Jesus, although they don't know what that means yet.

Advent is a season that is a borderland. A new year is coming. We're waiting for the coming of Jesus, both for his birth on Christmas Day and for his coming again on the Last Day.

New Year's is the usual time to examine our regrets and make plans to change for the better, but Advent starts us earlier. What from our past weighs us with guilt or shame? How we can seek forgiveness and make more room in a heavy heart for the coming of Christ? John the Baptist is fierce in his call to sinners, but often our sins and weaknesses are equally fierce in their hold on our lives. God invites us to repent and choose instead the fierceness of his love and grace.

Questions for Reflection

1. Does Advent feel like a strange time of year to ask for forgiveness? Why or why not?
2. Consider a way you might pursue repentance and forgiveness in your life. You might write a letter to God, arrange to talk with someone from whom you're estranged, talk to your pastor or priest, or consider a rite of reconciliation if your tradition practices it.

6. TURKISH DELIGHT

Why do you spend your money for that which is not bread,
and your labor for that which does not satisfy?
—Isaiah 55:2a

To follow along in the novel, read chapter 4.

After Edmund follows Lucy through the wardrobe, the White Witch discovers him, alone in the woods. She is suspicious at first but then offers him a place in her sleigh and something to eat. He asks for Turkish Delight, a candy snowy with powdered sugar, just like the snow of Narnia.

When Turkish Delight is fresh, it is nutty, chewy, creamy, and delicious, but it goes stale quickly, which makes it tough and tasteless. To understand what Edmund was craving, look for a high-end, vacuum-sealed box at a Middle Eastern grocery store (see suggested brands in session 2 of the Leader's Guide or in Narnia Night activities).

The Witch doesn't give Edmund real Turkish Delight. She gives him a kind of opiate, "this was enchanted Turkish Delight and . . . anyone who had once tasted it would want more and more of it." Edmund eats every last piece, trying to fill all the empty places inside himself.

What is real nourishment and what is junk food? What is real and what is illusion? The White Witch is beautiful and powerful, but she cares only about herself. The Witch's

Turkish Delight is delicious, but it leaves Edmund endlessly hungry for more. Later, Edmund finds he isn't interested in real food anymore; "he was thinking all the time about Turkish Delight—and there's nothing that spoils the taste of good ordinary food half so much as the memory of bad magic food."

Advertising, social media, or your own family may be working to convince you that there are certain expectations or products you need for a truly happy Christmas. But what will truly bring joy and what will be empty calories? Sometimes it's hard to tell, especially when we feel like Edmund—alone, uncomfortable, and hurting.

Questions for Reflection

1. What Christmas "junk food" may have caught your eye this year, offering an illusion of fun, happiness, or joy?
2. What things truly give sustenance to you or your family this time of year? Make a list of activities or traditions that increase a sense of God's grace in your life, rather than a sense of obligation, guilt, or "being a perfect family."
3. Consider how you can manage your stress levels this season to avoid making bad choices as Edmund did. For instance: slow down your schedule, let go of some holiday expectations, let go of a grudge, or simply fill your mind with "God is Love" or "Come, Lord Jesus," instead of "Hurry! Hurry!" or "Get it done!"

7. THE BREAD OF LIFE

Then Jesus said to them, "Very truly, I tell you, it was not Moses who gave you the bread from heaven, but it is my Father who gives you the true bread from heaven. For the bread of God is that which comes down from heaven and gives life to the world." They said to him, "Sir, give us this bread always."

Jesus said to them, "I am the bread of life. Whoever comes to me will never be hungry, and whoever believes in me will never be thirsty."
—John 6:32–35

The White Witch's candy, or "bad magic food" as Lewis calls it, makes Edmund lose his appetite for nourishment or "good ordinary food." Edmund develops a physical and spiritual addiction to the Witch's power and her magical Turkish Delight.

We all have "bad foods" we substitute for the good, whether it's junk food or anything else we use to avoid pain, fear, or emptiness. In the Christian life, our true food is the Bread of Life—the Eucharist and Jesus himself. The Bread of Life feeds us with love, hope, forgiveness, and community. With this true food, Jesus says, we will never go hungry.

Of course, there's being hungry and there's *being hungry.* A bit of bread and a sip of wine won't keep our bellies from growling. Starving families can't use faith to keep from starving to death if there's nothing to eat. The Eucharist is powerful, but it's not magic.

In this passage, Jesus is speaking to our deepest hungers and thirsts as human beings—for relationship, for meaning, for God. We may think we're hungrier for other things: security, beauty, respect, a happy family, job advancement. Or for tangible things such as French fries, Facebook, red wine, television, or exercise. None of these things are junk in and of themselves, but if we use them to feed our deepest hungers they can become "bad magic food" with no ability to truly satisfy us.

What does it mean, exactly, to feed ourselves with Jesus instead of junk food? It means we worship and receive Communion regularly, but it can also mean to reach out to a friend when we're struggling, to take a moment for prayer or to call on Jesus' name, to sleep well, to read the Bible, and to grow in our love of our friends and family. If we can make things like these our "good ordinary food," we will find fullness of life and nourishment in Christ and more easily turn away from "bad magic food."

Questions for Reflection

1. What might be some "bad magic foods" in your life right now?
2. Do you ever hunger for Jesus? What does that feel like?
3. What images come to you when you imagine Jesus as the Bread of Life? What could those images mean for your growth in your relationship with him?

WEEK TWO

8. LUCY

*"Ah, LORD God," I said, "I don't know how to speak
  because I'm only a child."
The LORD responded,
"Don't say, 'I'm only a child.'
  Where I send you, you must go;
  what I tell you, you must say.
Don't be afraid of them,
because I'm with you to rescue you,"
  declares the LORD.*
  —Jeremiah 1:6–8 (CEB)

To follow along in the novel, read chapters 1–2.

Lucy is the youngest Pevensie child, but she's also the family scout, prophet, and sage. Later, when she and her siblings become kings and queens of Narnia, she is known as Queen Lucy the Valiant. Lucy is brave not because she's big, strong, or tough but because she is curious, trusting, and imaginative.

When Lucy finds herself on the other side of the wardrobe, she doesn't run back. She doesn't even put on a fur coat to stay warm. She sees that Narnia is like her world, but not like it at all. It's nighttime, and there are trees covered with snow, although it was morning and springtime on the other side of the wardrobe door. She's full of wonder and walks into this strange forest to have a look around.

Lucy's wonder and trust guide her. She joins Mr. Tumnus, a nervous stranger with a tail and horns, for tea; something Peter, Susan, or Edmund would probably never have done. She convinces Peter and Susan to try to save Tumnus after he's been arrested. She is the first to see the Robin who leads her and her siblings to the Beavers.

Do curiosity and wonder play a part in faith? In *The Book of Common Prayer*, the prayer after baptism asks for the newly baptized: "an inquiring and discerning heart . . . and the gift of joy and wonder in all your works." In Scripture and in Narnia, these are clearly necessary for a life spent following God. May Lucy be an inspiration to you this season in her bravery, her sense of wonder, and her willingness to walk through an open door.

Questions for Reflection

1. We often feel unprepared, like Jeremiah, for what we are asked us to do, but Lucy doesn't let her lack of experience keep her from exploring Narnia. How has God helped you face a call or experience you didn't think you were ready for? How did that call or experience affect your life?

2. What about the Advent season most arouses your sense of wonder? What does that wonder lead you to want to explore? Are any "wardrobe doors" catching your attention right now?

9. THE PROFESSOR

"I believe; help my unbelief!" —Mark 9:24b

To follow along in the novel, read chapter 5.

C. S. Lewis knew that the biggest challenge of his Narnia books would be convincing readers that a fantasyland had something to teach them about Christianity. Magic wands, fauns, talking animals, and dryads aren't biblical, but they can surprise us into seeing the gospel in a new way. When we walk into Narnia, as Rowan Williams puts it, we enter "an unfamiliar world in which we could rediscover what it might mean to meet the holy without the staleness of religious preconceptions as they appear in our culture."[5] The strange and fantastic images and characters can also compel us to pay more attention to the power and meaning of the Christian story because our imaginations and emotions are freshly engaged.

In the novel, the Pevensie children stand in for us, and the ways we may experience Narnia (or Christianity) as readers. Lucy enters wholeheartedly. Peter and Susan struggle to believe. Edmund knows that there's something there, but he is too fearful and self-absorbed to admit it or fully enter (until later).

The older siblings worry about Lucy and decide to talk to the Professor, who owns the house where they're living. What can they do about their little sister? Is she going crazy? (They don't know it, and unless you've read *The Magician's Nephew*, you might not either, but the Professor has been to Narnia himself.) He gently, but pointedly, questions Susan and Peter about their reasons for not believing their sister. Why are they attached to such narrow definitions of reality?

Advent is a time to step into a world of imagination and wonder. It's easy to be cynical about the holidays, but if we can allow ourselves to feel some deep delight or let our imaginations run wild in the wonder or even the silliness of the season, we might be surprised into seeing both ourselves and God's world differently.

God was born among us to make what might seem ordinary or even crude to us (our bodies, poverty, a shared meal, suffering, death) into holy and transformative things. That can sound strange or crazy. So can a virgin birth, visiting angels, or magi! It can require imagination to enter into God's reality and to experience the Christmas season not as a silly, childish distraction, but as a radical new perspective on faith and the kingdom of God.

Questions for Reflection

1. Which Pevensie child are you most like, in terms of having faith in what you can't prove? Are you comfortable with this similarity or would you prefer to emulate one of the other children?

2. How does the season of Advent strain your sense of reason? Does it do so in a way that makes it difficult for you to enter fully into its meaning or relevance?

3. What are some ways that the season of Advent feeds your imagination? How does that affect your faith?

10. BECOMING LIKE CHILDREN

He called a child, whom he put among them, and said, "Truly I tell you, unless you change and become like children, you will never enter the kingdom of heaven." —Matthew 18:2–3

If we can't become like children in Advent, there may be no hope for us! Advent is one of the times of year when there is permission for adults to "play": decorating our homes, wearing colorful or goofy clothes, and reliving childhood holiday traditions. Even if our childhood holidays were unhappy, there are many ways to have the faith of a child in Advent. Advent wreaths, light displays, Christmas trees, nativity sets, cookie baking, or Secret Santa gift exchanges are all opportunities for the child within us to relearn the story of the birth of Christ through play and imagination.

My husband and I have no children, and we knew Christmas wouldn't be as fun unless we created special traditions of our own. I began collecting ornaments for a Jesse Tree. The Jesse Tree is a bare branch hung with symbols of stories from the Old Testament, creating a family "tree" for Mary, Joseph, and the Christ Child—a Christmas tree prequel! The name is from Isaiah, "A shoot shall come out from the stump of Jesse, / and a branch shall grow out of his roots" (Isa. 11:1). A Jesse Tree deepens my experience of Advent with play and Scripture. Each day I read a passage that reminds me of the long story of salvation leading to the birth of Jesus and hang a tiny ornament, like a globe (Creation), a well (Hagar in the desert), or a whale (Jonah).

Paraphrasing St. Paul's First Letter to the Corinthians, C. S. Lewis wrote in an essay: "When I became a man I put away childish things, including the fear of childishness and the desire to be very grown up."[6] The Narnia Chronicles and the season of Advent are opportunities for adults—including adults without children—to encounter faith, God, and the story of salvation in Christ through the eyes of children, whether it's in the magical wardrobe and talking animals of Narnia, a Christmas pageant, a nativity set, or a Jesse Tree.

Questions for Reflection

1. What do you think Jesus means by "become like children"?
2. What "childish" activities do you especially enjoy during Advent? If you haven't been in the habit of any such activities, which seem as if they would be fun to try, either this year or next?
3. C. S. Lewis also wrote, "Christ never meant that we were to remain children in intelligence: on the contrary. He told us to be not only 'as harmless as doves', but also 'as wise as serpents'. He wants a child's heart, but a grown-up's head."[7] What are some ways you can balance a "child's heart" and a "grown-up's head"? Do you think Lewis succeeds in balancing the two in *The Lion, the Witch, and the Wardrobe*? Why or why not?

11. EDMUND

⬤

For while we were still weak, at the right time Christ died for the ungodly. Indeed, rarely will anyone die for a righteous person—though perhaps for a good person someone might actually dare to die. But God proves his love for us in that while we still were sinners Christ died for us. —Romans 5:6–8

To follow along in the novel, read chapter 5.

Peter and Susan aren't always fair to Edmund, so he's often hurt and angry, feeling left behind and unappreciated. He is not a sympathetic character; he lies, he lashes out, and he turns against his family.

When Edmund follows Lucy into the wardrobe and sees Narnia, she is delighted. Later, he betrays her and denies Narnia's existence to Peter and Susan, "pretending. . . . Just for fun, of course. There's nothing there, really." When Edmund and his siblings tumble into Narnia together one afternoon, Peter calls him out on the lie. Edmund is furious and vows revenge.

So, he decides to betray his brother and sisters to the White Witch. He's a traitor, dishonest, and "a beast," as Peter calls him. Still, he's never lost to evil. His siblings love and worry about him. He feels a glimmer of compassion when the White Witch turns a Christmas party of small creatures to stone. He realizes that betraying his siblings to the Witch was a terrible mistake. Eventually, because of his sin and his humanity, it is for Edmund that Aslan gives his life.

We may identify more with Susan, Peter, or Lucy, but we all have something in common with Edmund. We have been guilty of dishonesty, selfishness, and betrayal, too. We are human. Like Edmund, regardless of what we have done: "unto us a child is born, unto us a son is given."(Isa. 9:6 KJV). Let us prepare our hearts to receive him, and bear fruits worthy of repentance (see Luke 3:8).

Questions for Reflection

1. What are some ways that you identify with Edmund? Do you see in yourself his desire for revenge, his unlikableness, his anger, or his loneliness?
2. Have you ever betrayed someone you loved? What happened? Have you experienced reconciliation, either with that person or with God?
3. Part of preparing our hearts for the coming of the Christ Child is reflecting on our past mistakes, betrayals, and sins. Write a letter to God confessing some of your most difficult wrongdoings. If you carry an especially difficult sin on your heart, consider asking to meet with your pastor or priest, perhaps for the rite of reconciliation if your tradition makes provision for it.

12. KEEPING AWAKE

[Jesus said,] "But in those days, after that suffering,
the sun will be darkened,
    and the moon will not give its light,
and the stars will be falling from heaven,
    and the powers in the heavens will be shaken.
. . . .
Therefore, keep awake—for you do not know when the master of
the house will come, in the evening, or at midnight, or at cockcrow,
or at dawn, or else he may find you asleep when he comes suddenly.
And what I say to you I say to all: Keep awake." —Mark 13:24-27,
35-37

The season of Advent watches and waits in two direc-
tions: first for Christ to be born, and second for Christ
to come again. There are many contrasts and parallels in
these two events. The birth of the baby Jesus comes on
earth in a sweet and humble stable, and Jesus promises to
return to earth at the end of time with power, earthquakes,
angels, and judgment. At his birth, there's a star in the East
beckoning the magi to the manger; at his second coming,
there will be stars falling from the sky while the sun and
moon go dark.

When Aslan returns to Narnia in the final book, *The
Last Battle*, there are stars that fall, a moon and sun that
are extinguished, and mountains that topple into the sea.
In *The Lion, the Witch, and the Wardrobe*, however, our wait-

ing is not for the end of time but for Aslan. The creatures of Narnia wait for him with longing, and their expectation is contagious; the three children (all but Edmund) are delighted in spite of themselves when Mr. Beaver first mentions Aslan's name.

Preparing ourselves to receive Jesus is about living our lives awake to hope, to love, and to our most needy neighbors. When ancient people wrote about *apocalypse*, what they described sounds despairing and destructive, but if we look a little deeper, those writers were trying to turn their worry and fear into hope. They were choosing to stay awake. We, too, must not fall asleep or numb ourselves but keep faith that God's love in Christ is more powerful than a brutal world.

As we wait for the coming of Jesus—at Christmas and on the Last Day—let us "keep awake" and practice hope, love, and justice as part of our daily lives. Not because we want to "be good" or earn our place in heaven, but because by so doing we will stay alert enough to meet Jesus whenever he appears before us.

Questions for Reflection

1. What are ways you can "keep awake" to justice this Advent? You might consider choosing a particular cause that speaks to your heart, praying for the people involved, and donating to a related charity.
2. What are ways you can "keep awake" to hope? You might consider making a list of things you worry about and writing next to each worry a hope you see for change or healing.
3. What are ways you can "keep awake" to love? You might consider prayerfully picturing yourself, a loved one, or even someone whom you consider an enemy, surrounded by a warm light of love and grace.

13. THE FUR COATS

Take off the garment of your sorrow and affliction, O Jerusalem,
and put on forever the beauty of the glory from God.
Put on the robe of the righteousness that comes from God;
put on your head the diadem of the glory of the Everlasting.
—Baruch 5:1–2

To follow along in the novel, read chapter 6.

As the Pevensie children walk through the wardrobe, they push past rows of fur coats before emerging outdoors into a cold and snowy forest. Susan, the responsible older sister, suggests they each put on a coat to keep warm in the Narnian winter weather. While her siblings sometimes criticize her for being bossy, Susan wants her family to prepare for whatever Narnia may bring before rushing out into the snow.

Advent is a season of preparation. At home, you may be decorating, listening to special music, wrapping, and baking. Your church may be lighting candles on an Advent wreath, rehearsing a pageant, or offering special programs or concerts. You may be hearing Scripture on Sundays from prophets, Jesus, and John the Baptist, warning and reassuring people about the times to come and what they should do to get ready.

Anticipation and preparation can be half the fun of an event or trip, but preparation—especially at this time of year—can become an end in itself and overwhelm any fun with to-do lists, guilt, and paranoia. Should Susan *also* have looked for boots and hats? A map? Should the children have turned back and packed a lunch? At some point, we have to let go of preparing and just step forward in faith.

Our Christmas preparations can take over Advent and leave little room to receive the Christ Child. Susan shows us that what we need may already be in front of us, if we are aware enough to notice. The fur coats were there when they needed them. The children meet others along the way who guide them and feed them. That doesn't mean that the journey is easy or that they're never cold, wet, or hungry; but, because they have one another and allow themselves to accept help from others, they have enough.

In the same way, throughout the Bible, God provides for God's people. Sometimes even with fur coats! After Adam and Eve are banished from the Garden of Eden, God provides them with "garments of skins" (Gen. 3:23) for warmth and protection. While the Israelites in the wilderness may have preferred cucumbers, wine, and beef, God provides them with manna, water, and pheasants.

Prepare is a traditional command for the season of Advent, but so are *Wait, Listen,* and *Watch.* Preparing to receive Christ into our hearts sometimes means that we prepare by doing less, not more.

Questions for Reflection

1. Reflect on a time when God unexpectedly provided what you needed, especially if you were not even aware of the need.
2. How is God providing what you need this Advent?
3. Is there something on your to-do list that you can let go of, having faith that God will provide for you?

14. ADAM AND EVE

And the LORD God made garments of skins for the man and for his wife, and clothed them. . . .

[T]he LORD God sent him forth from the garden of Eden, to till the ground from which he was taken. He drove out the man; and at the east of the garden of Eden he placed the cherubim, and a sword flaming and turning to guard the way to the tree of life. —Genesis 3:21, 23–24

The story of Adam and Eve is a Christmas story. The medieval church observed their feast day on December 24, as the necessary biblical backstory to the birth of Christ on December 25. Churches often held town-wide mystery plays of Creation, Adam and Eve, and the Nativity, among others, to commemorate the day and teach the story of salvation. The birth of humanity was a bookend in the liturgical year to the birth of Christ—in contrast, but also in parallel.

The story of Adam and Eve is an ancient story, but like so many passages in the Bible, it comes alive for us today because it's a story about being human. Adam and Eve probably sound strangely familiar to us. They point fingers at each other and at the snake. They won't take responsibility for what they've done. They hide from God. Although God is disappointed and angry that they can't seem to follow even simple commands, God still loves them. God sends them away from paradise to learn a few things about life—closing the door behind them—but God gives them clothes to wear on the way.

In Narnia, human children are called "Sons of Adam" and "Daughters of Eve," and, as it happens, the Pevensie children find fur coats in the wardrobe too, as they pass into a new world. Perhaps Adam and Eve face a greater danger than the White Witch, having to scratch their living from the dirt of the ground. Their new clothes are a sign of the end of paradise, where the Bible tells us they were vegetarians and went without clothes at all. The Pevensies' fur coats (too big for them) are a sign that they, too, will become new people one day, kings and queens of Narnia.

We've lived on the far side of paradise for generations now, and still, we don't do a very good job following God's commandments. Like Adam and Eve, we point fingers and hide from God. Even still, "unto us a child is born, unto us a son is given" (Isa. 9:6 KJV). God can't turn our lives back into paradise, but God offers God's own Son to us. God offers us new life and a new identity in Christ. And sometimes even a coat.

Questions for Reflection

1. Medieval Christians saw Adam and Eve and Jesus and Mary as matched pairs. Adam and Eve brought death to humanity; Jesus and Mary brought life. What are some other ways you might compare and contrast them?

2. The story of the Fall is one of the most well known in the Bible. Why do you think this is? Does the story of the Fall speak to your life?

WEEK THREE

15. LIKE A THIEF

$\infty\!\bigcirc$

Now concerning the times and the seasons, brothers and sisters, you do not need to have anything written to you. For you yourselves know very well that the day of the Lord will come like a thief in the night.
—*1 Thessalonians 5:1–2*

It sounds frightening to imagine Jesus returning like a burglar or prowler, sneaking around our lives and trying to break in by force. During Advent, we hear a number of somewhat disturbing Scripture readings on Sundays, describing Jesus' return at the second coming (see Luke 21:34–35 or 2 Pet. 3:9–10a, for example).

There's a lot of sneaking around in *The Lion, the Witch, and the Wardrobe*, too. The children sneak around the Professor's house, playing hide and seek. Tumnus sneaks Lucy back to the lamppost, trying to escape the detection of the White Witch. A robin surreptitiously leads the children to safety through the woods. Edmund sneaks away from dinner to find the Witch's castle. The Beavers and children sneak away through a snowstorm to hide in a secret cave, evading the Witch. Even Aslan himself is "on the move," making his approach behind the scenes, sneaking around the boundaries of Narnia while choosing when he will emerge for all to see.

Can "sneaking" be positive? What about parents hiding presents from their kids and filling stockings, leaving cookie crumbs behind on Christmas Eve while children sleep? Could Christ's sneaky return be both alarming but also a delightful relief? God's ways are stealthy and mysterious to human beings, and yet we must trust that God is about love, redemption, and grace. Rowan Williams puts it this way: "In a word, what Lewis portrays with such power and freshness in Narnia is simply *grace*: the unplanned and uncontrolled incursion into our self-preoccupied lives of God's joy in himself."[8]

The powers of evil and sin are sneaky, too. Why shouldn't Christ also sneak about with secrecy and care to trick and overturn the plans and powers of spiritual forces that seek to hurt and destroy? Or do some skulking around in the crawlspaces and locked drawers of our souls and bodies, where he might be able to free us from some of our sin and shame?

Come quickly, Lord Jesus, even now, and break open our lives and our world to your sneaky, powerful grace.

Questions for Reflection

1. What is frightening for you when you imagine Christ's second coming? What would be alarming? What would be a relief?
2. Are there ways you've noticed Christ's grace trying to sneak into your life lately?

16. THE ROBIN

~ ◠◡◠ ~

Let me hear of your steadfast love in the morning,
for in you I put my trust.
Teach me the way I should go,
for to you I lift up my soul.

—*Psalm 143:8*

To follow along in the novel, read chapter 6.

After discovering that Lucy's friend Tumnus has been arrested, the children are a bit shaken. But a beautiful robin gets Lucy's attention and seems to want to lead them somewhere. As Lewis puts it, "You couldn't find a robin with a redder breast or a brighter eye." To three of the Pevensie children, the Robin is clearly trustworthy. They decide to follow.

Edmund tries to convince Peter to doubt the Robin and everything about Narnia. "Which side *is* the right side? How do we know that the Fauns are in the right and the Queen . . . in the wrong?" His judgment has been clouded by fear and greed; he doesn't see in the same way his siblings do.

All kinds of beautiful robins hop across our path each December; some lead us in the way we should go while others end up being just shiny glass or useless sawdust. In Advent, with its consumer bonanza, busy schedules, short days, and long nights, we can get disoriented. To make it more complicated, the choices we're trying to make are often between two *good* choices, rather than a good one and a bad one. Should I go to that holiday party or stay home and read a book about prayer? Should I indulge a little Christmas spontaneity and buy that festive but expensive tablecloth, or buy a few extra presents for others? Should I spend an afternoon visiting my niece and nephew across town, or join a church group at the soup kitchen?

There are more monumental choices we must make, of course. Whether the choice is serious or not, what we are deciding is who we will be and where we will place our trust. There is not a "right" decision in choosing whether to put your trust in a party or a book, except in your own heart. But in choosing whether to follow Aslan or the White Witch, Edmund later sees that he has placed trust in someone even more greedy and fearful than he is, who cares nothing about him and might well leave him for dead.

Back in the forest, Peter isn't swayed by Edmund's cynicism. The Professor's words to him have taken root; he trusts his judgment and past experience, that robins are "good birds in all the stories I've ever read."

God gives us an inner voice, too, and previous experiences to help us make the right choices and trust the right people. And we have communities and loved ones to help if we're still uncertain.

Questions for Reflection

1. Make a list of what you feel you "ought" to do this Advent and a list of what you "want" to do. What are the motivations behind the two lists? If they are out of balance, how could you better balance them?
2. What signs, feelings, or urgings do you trust or follow when making serious decisions in your life?

17. ANGELS AND MESSENGERS

In the sixth month the angel Gabriel was sent by God to a town in Galilee called Nazareth, to a virgin engaged to a man whose name was Joseph, of the house of David. The virgin's name was Mary. And he came to her and said, "Greetings, favored one! The Lord is with you." But she was much perplexed by his words and pondered what sort of greeting this might be. The angel said to her, "Do not be afraid, Mary, for you have found favor with God." —Luke 1:26–30

Advent is a season of angels—Gabriel appears to Mary, Joseph, and Zechariah; a heavenly host appears to the shepherds on Christmas night—but there are no angels in Narnia. Perhaps this is a bit surprising in a land of unicorns, naiads, and wraiths, but for the most part Lewis avoids overtly biblical figures or imagery in his Narnia books.

In both Hebrew and Greek, the word for *angel* is the same as the word for *messenger*. Angels have many ways of serving God, according to Scripture, and carrying messages to human beings is an important one.

The Robin is very much like an angel, a winged messenger in the service of Aslan, guiding the children to safety and help but also calling them to follow Aslan, even though they don't even know his name yet. Like Mary, they say yes, even though they cannot know what lies ahead. They have seen Tumnus's cave, destroyed by the Witch's police, so they know that danger is close. They put themselves in the Robin's hands, forgetting about dinner and home, because they want to see where he will lead them.

Mary, too, told Gabriel yes without knowing much about where she was being led, beyond the goodness and love of the God who was leading her. May we remain open to God's messengers in our lives, too, whether they arrive in the form of birds, friends, or a glorious heavenly host.

Questions for Reflection

1. Have you ever had a feeling you'd been visited by an angel? What made you feel that way? Did you ever tell anyone else?
2. Have you ever felt God leading you in a direction you didn't expect? What were the messengers or clues that signaled this to you? Did you end up following in that unexpected path or not? Why or why not?

18. MR. AND MRS. BEAVER

For as often as you eat this bread and drink the cup, you proclaim the Lord's death until he comes. — *1 Corinthians 11:26*

To follow along in the novel, read chapters 7–8.

Mr. Beaver finds the children in the woods and takes them home to Mrs. Beaver, where they help prepare a meal. Mr. Beaver and Peter go fishing while Mrs. Beaver and the girls spread the table. Then, in one of the coziest passages in the novel, they all sit down together and eat a meal of fried fish, potatoes with butter, hot cups of tea, and a "great and gloriously sticky marmalade roll." (See appendix B for a recipe if you'd like to try it.)

When everyone is fed, Mr. Beaver says, "Why, now we can get to business." It is then that children become part of the movement to bring Aslan back to Narnia; one in which, although they don't realize it yet, they will play a central role.

Meeting the Beavers is the major turning point for the children. The Beavers welcome them with great hospitality into their home and to Narnia. They are fed, physically and spiritually. They learn about Aslan. They truly become part of the kingdom of Narnia — the kingdom of Aslan.

The Beavers' dinner is also where Edmund decides to leave his family and join the White Witch. He feels unsatisfied, hungry for Turkish Delight (the "bad magic food" that makes "good ordinary food" unsatisfactory). Like Judas at the Last Supper, he slips out, unable to share in the hospitality and Communion, betrayal on his mind. He can't receive the Beavers' welcome or the good news of Aslan's coming.

When the Beavers and his siblings see that Edmund has left, they realize that they are in great danger. The Witch's forces will come after them. A snowstorm is raging. The meal they've prepared and shared has brought them together and strengthened them for what is to come.

Advent and Christmas are seasons we celebrate with meals and eating. Remember to feed yourself well, with good food and loving company. Jesus often shared meals with others as part of his ministry on earth, and he continues to share himself with us through the bread and the cup of the eucharistic meal. But he is also with us in any meal of love and Communion we share. May your meals and feasts this season strengthen you to face the storms raging in your own life and prepare you to receive Christ and his love this Christmas.

Questions for Reflection

1. What are some ways you can make an ordinary meal more of a communion with God? You might consider lighting a candle, reflecting on moments of gratitude, playing special music, or connecting with an old friend.
2. Is there any resentment or grief in your life that could be keeping you from receiving the hospitality of God or your loved ones? What could help you stay at the table and receive hospitality?

19. CHRISTMAS AND EUCHARIST

While they were eating, Jesus took a loaf of bread, and after blessing it he broke it, gave it to the disciples, and said, "Take, eat; this is my body." Then he took a cup, and after giving thanks he gave it to them, saying, "Drink from it, all of you; for this is my blood of the covenant, which is poured out for many for the forgiveness of sins." —Matthew 26:26–28

I worshiped at an Episcopal church for the first time on a Christmas Eve, years ago. Many things were new to me, but I remember especially the strange feeling that, on the night when we were celebrating Jesus as a tiny baby, we were also hearing and celebrating that "on the night before he died, our Lord Jesus Christ took bread." Maundy Thursday, Good Friday, and Christmas all stood next to each other.

What does Communion have to do with Christmas? Your church may or may not celebrate Communion on Christmas Eve, but that night we do all celebrate that God has come to earth. That in Jesus, God was born to live and to die as one of us, for us.

When he offered his disciples bread and wine at the Last Supper, Jesus called them his body and blood, a shocking statement. C. S. Lewis wrote, "I don't know and can't imagine what the disciples understood our Lord to mean when, His body still unbroken and His blood unshed, He handed them the bread and wine, saying they were His body and blood"; and yet, "the command, after all, was Take, eat: not Take, understand."[9] This was a true meal, not just an idea. Jesus was truly human and truly God, not just a metaphor.

Perhaps this is why Lewis chose a lion as the savior for Narnia. A lion has a formidable body: large, strong, thick with fur. Lions have big teeth and claws, and sometimes they eat people. Jesus, like Aslan, is embodied, powerful, and real; not a beam of light or puff of wind.

In the stable on Christmas Eve, we will see his body, lying in a manger. He was a real baby. He had a physical birth and died a physical death. And he offers himself to us, even when we don't know how to receive him.

Questions for Reflection

1. Have you experienced a Communion liturgy in the Advent season or on Christmas Eve? How did it feel to you? What connections or disconnects did you experience?
2. Is it important for you to feel that you understand what Communion (or the Eucharist) means? Why or why not?
3. What makes Jesus feel physically real to you? Does that matter to your faith?

20. THE WITCH'S HOUSE

*A new heart I will give you, and a new spirit I will put within you; and
I will remove from your body the heart of stone and give you a heart
of flesh. —Ezekiel 36:26*

To follow along in the novel, read chapter 9.

After Edmund slips away, leaving his siblings and the
Beavers at dinner, he realizes he's forgotten his coat.
He walks through the snowstorm, shivering and cold,
toward the Witch's house. He considers turning around,
but when he thinks of becoming king, his heart warms
with thoughts of power, luxury, and revenge against his
brother. He pushes on.

Inside the castle's iron gate is a courtyard full of statues,
creatures the Witch has turned to stone. Then Edmund
trips over Maugrim, the only living creature he meets
there, a ferocious wolf. Maugrim takes him to the throne
room, where there are more statues and the White Witch
sitting alone in the gloom.

Edmund thought he would find glory, revenge, and
Turkish Delight when he reached her castle. Instead, he
gets scorn and a piece of stale bread. This is where fear and
revenge lead us, Lewis seems to say. The White Witch's
house is a castle, but no palace; it's a dim, cold storage

locker of statues. One lamp shines over the Witch's shoulder, illuminating little else.

James Baldwin once wrote, "I imagine one of the reasons people cling to their hates so stubbornly is because they sense, once hate is gone, they will be forced to deal with pain."[10] Edmund would much rather focus on hating his brother than on his own pain. His hate seems to take the place of a coat in the blustering snowstorm. So, too, the White Witch has frozen Narnia so that nothing can challenge or hurt her. Long before Narnia was created, she destroyed her kingdom and killed her own sister rather than accept defeat.

God will not keep us away from the pain of human life. The baby Jesus was born in a cave, poor and exposed. God walked into the middle of human pain and rage and was willingly crucified, and so there is no need for us to be afraid of pain, danger, or death. In Christ, God pitches his tent (no castle) in our midst and is called Emmanuel— "God with us."

Questions for Reflection

1. In what other ways is the Witch's house similar to the nature of her rule?
2. Are there ways you over-insulate yourself from harm or danger? Are there valuable experiences or relationships you might be missing as a result of this?
3. Is there someone in your life on whom you often focus blame or even hatred? Where does this blame or hate lead you?

21. THE HOUSE OF DAVID

But that same night the word of the LORD came to Nathan: Go and tell my servant David: Thus says the LORD: Are you the one to build me a house to live in? I have not lived in a house since the day I brought up the people of Israel from Egypt to this day, but I have been moving about in a tent and a tabernacle. . . . Moreover the LORD declares to you that the LORD will make you a house. . . . Your house and your kingdom shall be made sure forever before me; your throne shall be established forever. —2 Samuel 7:4–6, 11b, 16

There is a verse easy to overlook in the story of the Annunciation (Luke 1:26–28), when Gabriel tells Mary about her child-to-be, "the Lord God will give to him the throne of his ancestor David." Mary, however, would have known how important this was, that her baby would fulfill the promise God made to King David, generations before. God promised security and stability to his people through David, whose rule over the people of Israel and Judah would be eternal, held by a dynasty that would never die out.

The House of David as a seat of power, like the Witch's castle in Narnia, eventually broke apart. As a house of relationships, however, it stayed intact in the faith of the Jewish people. God told David through the prophet Nathan, "the LORD will make you a house," and God meant that David, and all Israel, are a house and throne for Godself.

When God came to earth as Christ, Jesus became that house. The Jewish people saw the Temple too as God's house on earth, and Jesus spoke of his body as the new Temple. St. Paul writes, "Do you not know that you are God's temple and that God's Spirit dwells in you?" (1 Cor. 3:16). Jesus also taught that each of us is a house for God, saying, "Abide in me as I abide in you" (John 15:4).

C. S. Lewis, borrowing from George MacDonald, wrote beautifully about this in his book, *Mere Christianity:*

> Imagine yourself as a living house. God comes in to rebuild that house. At first, perhaps, you can understand what He is doing. He is getting the drains right and stopping the leaks in the roof and so on; you knew that those jobs needed doing and so you are not surprised. But presently He starts knocking the house about in a way that hurts abominably and does not seem to make any sense. What on earth is He up to? The explanation is that He is building quite a different house from the one you thought of—throwing out a new wing here, putting on an extra floor there, running up towers, making courtyards. You thought you were being made into a decent little cottage: but He is building a palace. He intends to come and live in it Himself.[11]

Questions for Reflection

1. Churches are also meant to be safe and inviting places to encounter and deepen our relationships with God. How is your church living out its ministry as a house for God and God's people? How you could you play more of a role in that ministry?
2. Using the quotation from C. S. Lewis, reflect on ways that God is building you into a palace for Godself.

WEEK FOUR

22. IS HE SAFE?

See, I am sending my messenger to prepare the way before me, and the Lord whom you seek will suddenly come to his temple. The messenger of the covenant in whom you delight—indeed, he is coming, says the LORD of hosts. But who can endure the day of his coming, and who can stand when he appears?

For he is like a refiner's fire and like fullers' soap; he will sit as a refiner and purifier of silver, and he will purify the descendants of Levi and refine them like gold and silver, until they present offerings to the LORD in righteousness. —Malachi 3:1–3

One of the most famous quotes from *The Lion, the Witch, and the Wardrobe* is Mr. Beaver's response to Susan and Lucy's nervous question about Aslan: "Is he safe?" Mr. Beaver answers, " 'Course he isn't safe. But he's good. He's the King" (chap. 8).

The passage from Malachi describes a messenger of judgment, whom Christians traditionally interpret as Christ. This is not a sweet baby Jesus. He's more like an avenging angel (or a ferocious lion?). His mission isn't to avenge or punish but to purify and restore, which are, frankly, painful. Silver was burned and refined by fire; wool was cleaned and whitened with harsh soap and rough paddling. Reconciliation can bring great relief, but it's a rough process.

The birth of Jesus would have been a painful but joyful experience for Mary and Joseph. Their baby was born under difficult circumstances and in a lonely place, far from friendly faces or the help of people they loved. Still, he was their baby boy, their firstborn son; and they knew he would become a light to the nations.

Jesus' second coming will be both joyful and fearsome, too. Who won't be glad to see things made new and put right? But . . . what will it cost? What will be changed and refined in us? Will it hurt? How much? Jesus is not safe, but like Aslan, "he's good," and "he's the King."

Like waiting for a child to be born, like waiting for Christmas Day to come, like waiting for Aslan to appear, it's both exciting and daunting to wait for Christ's return. Regardless of how we feel about it, he will return one day to restore the world and redeem us, ready or not.

Questions for Reflection

1. Do you think much about the second coming? What's it like to imagine Jesus' returning one day as a reality, rather than as described by a movie plot or fringe religious sect?

2. What in you might be in need of "refining"? How might it hurt? How might it be a relief?

3. Is it more challenging for you to imagine Christ as a dangerous bringer of judgment or as a loving, merciful redeemer? Why do you think that is?

23. FATHER CHRISTMAS

*Now there are varieties of gifts, but the same Spirit; . . .
[t]o each is given the manifestation of the Spirit for the
common good. —1 Corinthians 12:4, 7*

To follow along in the novel, read chapter 10.

Peter, Susan, Lucy, and the Beavers are on their way to
Aslan's camp when they meet Father Christmas. While
Santa Claus seems to either delight children or scare them
to death, Father Christmas is different. Sure, he wears a
red, fur-trimmed coat and has brought gifts, but he doesn't
laugh like a bowl full of jelly or eat cookies with the children. He doesn't terrify them, either, but they are certainly
in awe of him. Lewis describes him: "He was so big, and so
glad, and so real, that they all became quite still. They felt
very glad, but also solemn."

In Narnia, the time of "winter but never Christmas" has
ended. Christmas in Narnia is serious business; it's a sign of
victory against the White Witch. Father Christmas is less
like Santa Claus than John the Baptist, sharing the news
that a new time has come in which to get ready because the
rightful king is on his way.

He tells the children their gifts are "tools, not toys." He
gives them things that would make a Parent Safety Board
raise an eyebrow. For Peter, a sword and shield. For Susan,

a bow, a quiver of arrows, and a horn to blow in times of danger. For Lucy, medicine and a dagger. The gifts call their individual personalities and talents to join Aslan in fighting the power of the White Witch. They won't be called to do more than they're capable of, and yet, even as children, they are taken seriously as participants of Aslan's kingdom.

Being ready for Christmas and the birth of Jesus is about joy but also about courage. God is with us, and God also calls us to live in Christ, here and now. God calls us to stand for goodness and kindness, to stand against "might makes right," to choose joy, patience, faith, and self-control (see Gal. 5), to join in the struggle of the gospel to rout evil from the world. Be brave, knowing that God has equipped you with gifts and practical tools to make a difference in the world and that Jesus comes among us to lead us in that struggle.

Questions for Reflection

1. Which of Father Christmas's gifts to the children are you most drawn to? How might that gift match your own gifts and talents, the ways God has called you to help bring the good news of God's love into the world?
2. Why do you think Father Christmas has no gift for Edmund, even for his siblings to hold on to for him, when later in the novel, he's redeemed and joins in the fight?

24. THE FULL ARMOR OF GOD

Put on the whole armor of God, so that you may be able to stand against the wiles of the devil. For our struggle is not against enemies of blood and flesh, but against the rulers, against the authorities, against the cosmic powers of this present darkness, against the spiritual forces of evil in the heavenly places. Therefore take up the whole armor of God, so that you may be able to withstand on that evil day, and having done everything, to stand firm. Stand therefore, and fasten the belt of truth around your waist, and put on the breastplate of righteousness. As shoes for your feet put on whatever will make you ready to proclaim the gospel of peace. With all of these, take the shield of faith, with which you will be able to quench all the flaming arrows of the evil one. Take the helmet of salvation, and the sword of the Spirit, which is the word of God. —Ephesians 6:11–17

Father Christmas arms Peter, Susan, and Lucy with armor and weapons to stand against the White Witch. They are only children, but they're ready for battle. Sometimes, human beings must take up real weapons to fight for justice or "against the wiles of the devil," but more often, our Christian ethics mean, as Paul encourages us, that we will choose instead to fight with truth, righteousness, faith, Scripture, and the Gospel.

Advent is a time for making peace but also for standing against injustice and shining light into places of darkness and sin in our world. Preparing the way for Christ isn't something we do only in the privacy of our own hearts but in our communities and across the world. Paul reminds us that God's armor isn't to be used against other human beings but against the "spiritual forces of evil." But it's much harder to know what it means to swing a sword of the Spirit against the devil than to read about Edmund and Peter wielding literal swords against the evil army of the White Witch.

Scripture shows us that the strengths God chooses to anoint do not spring from raw, brute power but from virtues such as faith, cleverness, wisdom, or humility. The armor of God doesn't make us look like a bunch of medieval knights so much, to use a few scriptural examples, as an old man and his wife traveling across the desert, a sly kid who tricks his older brother out of a birthright, a prisoner interpreting dreams, or a young woman agreeing to sacrifice her reputation and possibly her fiancée because God has asked her to carry a child out of wedlock.

Like the Pevensie children, we're not expected to carry every item of spiritual defense at all times. But preparing ourselves and our communities for the Savior means taking seriously our call to stand against evil and injustice, whether our armor is a skill with words or skill in actions, the financial resources to make gifts to charity, or the inner resources to stand up at a protest or at a school board meeting. Take the armor God has given you seriously and prepare the way of the Lord, that "all the ends of the earth shall see the salvation of our God" (Isa. 52:10).

Questions for Reflection

1. What "battles" or causes need to be fought for in your town, neighborhood, or workplace? What issue is important enough to you to fight for it?
2. What weapons or armor has God given you to stand against injustice and evil in your community?

25. A TINY FEAST

Why do you spend your money for that which is not bread,
and your labor for that which does not satisfy?
Listen carefully to me, and eat what is good,
and delight yourselves in rich food.

—Isaiah 55:2

To follow along in the novel, read chapter 10.

Edmund is freezing cold (still with no coat) as he, the White Witch, and her dwarf jostle over the snow in her sleigh, scrambling to find the other children now that they know Aslan is on the move. Edmund now has a sinking feeling about the Witch; she hasn't offered him any Turkish Delight, only stale bread, and she treats him as a prisoner. "It didn't look now as if the Witch intended to make him a King," he thinks to himself.

In fact, the Witch's reign, where "it's winter but never Christmas," is starting to give way. Edmund doesn't realize it, but Father Christmas has found his siblings. The Witch's sleigh stumbles on another party Father Christmas has visited, a group of small forest creatures seated at a Christmas supper table in the middle of the woods. Edmund is hungry, and their tiny feast smells delicious.

The White Witch is outraged. When she finds out that

it's Father Christmas who has given them the feast, she turns the whole supper party to stone. Edmund is horrified. He sees the Witch, finally, for who she really is.

She is furious to hear that anyone is celebrating what ostensibly means the end of her reign, but she also is indignant at the existence of a feast at all. She shouts, "What is the meaning of all this gluttony, this waste, this self-indulgence?" A feast is a waste, no matter what it celebrates. No one in her kingdom should be enjoying physical pleasure or comfort. Even the Queen herself, aside from a few furs and a crown, seems to own nothing luxurious or pleasurable. Her castle is bare as a tomb.

Her disdain for luxury is a stark contrast to the Beavers, who serve a delectable meal (including dessert) to the children. Aslan sets up his military camp with a beautiful tent pavilion of yellow and crimson. The kingdom of God is a place of honesty and uprightness but also a place for delicious meals, physical comforts, and beauty. Advent is a time for both repentance and waiting, and it is also a time to celebrate the goodness of creation. Embrace the beauty and richness of the created world God has given us and to which he came, incarnate, that first Christmas.

Questions for Reflection

1. In Christianity, both fasting and feasting have been traditional spiritual practices. Have you ever considered that "feasting" in Advent or at Christmas (cookies, chocolate, smoked salmon, champagne, etc.) could be a celebration of the coming of Christ rather than just an indulgence or lapse in your diet?

2. Why is being a miser, like the White Witch, counter to the love and grace of God in Christ?

26. GOD WILL PREPARE A FEAST

On this mountain the Lord of hosts will make for all peoples
a feast of rich food, a feast of well-matured wines,
of rich food filled with marrow, of well-matured wines
strained clear.

. . . .

It will be said on that day,
Lo, this is our God; we have waited for him, so that he might
save us.
This is the Lord for whom we have waited;
let us be glad and rejoice in his salvation.

—Isaiah 25:6, 9

After a time of great destruction, Isaiah imagines a feast spread out by God for people who have suffered terrible violence and deprivation. The people have nothing left, so God provides everything. Imagine refugees from a modern war finding a heavy banquet table in the middle of nowhere, set with fine wines and the best food they've ever eaten. If the question is, "Can God spread a table in the wilderness?" (Ps. 78:19), the answer is yes.

The creatures of Narnia, like the people Isaiah knows and like the survivors of any war, have also survived a time of violence and loss. The White Witch has covered their land with ice and snow and turned dissenters into statues. She frowns on feasting, calling it a "waste." As the power of her winter is diminishing, Father Christmas arrives not only with gifts for the children and the Beavers but also with a table set with hot tea and china cups. For some woodland folk, he spreads a Christmas table in the forest with a hot supper, decorations, plum pudding, and wine. Father Christmas is helping the Narnians to remember life before the coming of the White Witch and to celebrate the new time that is coming.

When we gather during Advent and Christmas (or any special time), no matter what hurt or broken relationships have gone before, friends and family are put back together with a good meal. A feast doesn't erase mistakes or betrayals, but it can remind us who God created us to be and that Christ has redeemed us.

A special family meal isn't a promise that nothing will ever go wrong again. The people of Isaiah's time would be torn apart by war and sent away into exile. In Narnia, the Christmas supper party would be turned to stone. But the people of Israel knew that God was with them, no matter what, and that God's promises to them were eternal. The woodland creatures know that Aslan is on his way, even as the Witch raises her wand (the Witch knows, too!). We celebrate with parties and feasts now, knowing that they are a foretaste of God's redemption still to come.

Questions for Reflection

1. What would be set on the table if God were to "spread a table in the wilderness" for you? Make a list of foods, beverages, and decorations.
2. What are holiday family meals like for you? Do tension, celebration, and grace play equal roles? Are there ways you could bring more grace to meals in your family?

27. ASLAN IS NEAR

But you, O Bethlehem of Ephrathah,
who are one of the little clans of Judah,
from you shall come forth for me
one who is to rule in Israel,
whose origin is from of old,
from ancient days.

—*Micah 5:2*

To follow along in the novel, read chapter 11.

Aslan is near. In Narnia, Father Christmas has come, winter is disappearing, and even Edmund is ready to be free of the rule of the White Witch. Her final destruction will come later, but her stranglehold on Narnia is slowly coming undone.

The Witch's power is coming apart because of Aslan, who is stealthily returning to the land he created. But she is also being foiled by the faith and perseverance of a group of otherwise small and humble creatures who have been surviving under her tyranny: Mr. Tumnus, the Beavers, the Robin, a fox, squirrels, satyrs, and mice. Their watching and waiting have prepared the way for Aslan's coming.

The arrival of the four Pevensie children filled the Narnians with hope and expectation because a prophecy had said that four humans would bring Aslan's return. Susan, Peter, Edmund, and Lucy weren't quite sure what they were doing in Narnia or what was happening there, but they chose to become part of the community they found, anyway (although it took Edmund a little longer). Christmas came to Narnia because of those small animals and the four children: their faith, their willingness to change and repent, and their love and care for one another.

The first Christmas came because of the power of God but also because of the willingness of ordinary people to prepare the way. Mary, Joseph, Elizabeth, Zechariah, some shepherds, and an innkeeper were watching, waiting, and willing to be part of God's plan. Advent means the same for us: watching, waiting, and finding ways to enter into God's plan.

Jesus is coming. He will not be born as a warrior king, a giant, or a lion, but as a tiny human baby. He will melt the power of sin, evil, and death. However, the work of God's vulnerable but powerful love is also in our hands, now and until the day that Jesus will return.

Questions for Reflection

1. In what ways might your congregation be similar to a small band of forest animals and children? How could this be a strength? How could this be a weakness?
2. What small role might you be playing to help Christ come into the world?
3. In Scripture, God often chooses the small, the underdog, or the younger brother as a leader or change agent. Why do you think that could be?

28. THE WINTER IS PAST

[F]or now the winter is past,
the rain is over and gone.
The flowers appear on the earth;
the time of singing has come,
and the voice of the turtledove
is heard in our land.
—*Song of Solomon 2:1–12*

In Narnia, where it was "always winter but never Christmas," winter has ended. Father Christmas has come. The snow has melted, there are snowdrops, crocuses, and primroses blooming. The birds are singing, and trees are putting out tiny green leaves. A long, terrible winter is over, and the White Witch is on the run. Her sled has become useless, so she must walk. Finally, her dwarf declares: "This is no thaw. This is *spring*. What are we to do? Your winter has been destroyed, I tell you! This is Aslan's doing" (see chap. 11 in the novel).

Christmas has come for us too. But while snow may or may not be melting in your neck of the woods, nowhere on earth is it astronomical springtime. Summer has begun in the southern hemisphere and winter is enfolding the north. Nevertheless, Christmas feels like springtime, whether it's the darkest time of the winter or days stretched their longest. We are filled with the same joy and anticipation in new life we feel at the return of the first green shoots and warm days of spring. Jesus has come, and a new age is begun; Jesus will return and remake the world forever.

With Aslan's coming, winter's grip has been destroyed. With Jesus' birth, sin's power is on the run. "This is no thaw. This is *spring*."

Merry Christmas!

Questions for Reflection

1. Are there other ways that Christmas could be like the coming of spring?
2. What new things, in particular, may Christmas be bringing into your life this year?

SESSIONS FOR SMALL GROUP DISCUSSION

A LEADER'S GUIDE

Session 1 — The Wardrobe   *Session 3 — Father Christmas*
Session 2 — The Witch   *Session 4 — The Lion*

This discussion series works best if participants have read the novel (or at least chapters 1–5) or seen a movie version before participating. However, it is still accessible to people who can't manage doing either at this busy time of year.

There are four sessions, but in the case of a shorter Advent season, you may wish to omit session 3.

For each session, the materials you need are:

1. at least one copy of the novel (no photocopies; see below)
2. a newsprint pad and easel (optional)
3. for session 2, a box of Turkish Delight
4. if you choose, a movie version (see appendix A for details on the three most commonly available), DVD player, and television, screen, or other means of projection (see copyright restrictions, below)

I offer discussion questions with possible answers listed below each, but as your group starts talking, group interest and the Holy Spirit may choose other points for discussion and inquiry. Don't feel as if you have to follow the outline to the letter.

About Copyright

The Lion, the Witch, and the Wardrobe is still under copyright. The number of pages required for this study series exceeds Fair Use standards, so you may not make photocopies. You can pass a copy of the book around to read aloud or encourage people to bring their own copy. You may show a movie version in this context without permission as long as participation is restricted to people in your church and not advertised to the public. This is considered a face-to-face teaching activity; however, you must be using a legitimate, purchased copy of the movie (17 U.S.C. § 110(1)).

SESSION 1: THE WARDROBE

Gathering

Welcome everyone. Open with prayer.
Invite those gathered to go around the circle and share:
   —their names
   —whether they've read *The Lion, the Witch, and the Wardrobe* and how long ago
   —why they've come to this Advent study

Opening Discussion

The Chronicles of Narnia were written to stand alone as adventure and fantasy stories, but they can also be read on a deeper level with underlying Christian themes. Had you known that Lewis wrote with a Christian theme in mind? If you've read the series before, was this noticeable to you? Why or why not?

What are some themes we find in both Advent and *The Lion, the Witch, and the Wardrobe*?
   watching and waiting for Aslan or Christ to appear, light and darkness, snow (in some parts of the world), visit from Father Christmas / Santa . . .

Entering the Story

Reading Aloud
Start in chapter 1, with "This must be a simply enormous wardrobe!" and continue into chapter 2, ending with Mr. Tumnus saying, "I should no doubt know all about those strange countries. It is too late now."

You may want to ask participants to take turns reading by sentence or paragraph around the circle (inviting multiple readers is a good way to keep everyone engaged with what they're hearing). You can tell people they may "pass" if they would rather not read aloud.

Optional Movie Clip
Watch together the scene where Lucy goes through the wardrobe and finds the lamppost in the woods. Stop when she meets Mr. Tumnus. (Use any movie version.)

Reflection on the Story
Invite participants to share what they notice about the scene. Was there anything they were particularly drawn to? Anything they disliked? Compare the movie version to the book version of the scene between Lucy and Tumnus, if you're using both.

What do you notice about Lucy as the center of this scene?
she's very young, she's confident, she's not afraid, she's curious . . .

What Advent themes do you notice in this scene?
snow, Tumnus's arms are full of packages (like Christmas gifts), lamppost: a light in the darkness, entering a different and magical world, anticipation . . .

Deeper Discussion

1. "Strive to enter through the narrow door; for many, I tell you, will try to enter and will not be able" (Luke 13:24). Read the verse to the group or have them find it in their Bibles. How can you relate this passage about Christ and Christians to Lucy passing through the wardrobe into Narnia? What are some similarities? What are some differences?
2. Have there been wardrobe doors in your life that have led to greater experiences of faith or of God? Think about a place, experience, book, or time in your life that felt somehow set apart, spiritual, or even magical.
3. Is Advent usually a time of spiritual growth for you? Why or why not?

Closing Prayer

God of Hope, as we walk through the door of the season of Advent, watching and waiting for your Son, journey with us. Give us a sense of wonder at your works and in your love for all creation. Give us courage to deepen our faith as we face the busy schedules and heightened expectations of the season. All this we ask in the name of Jesus Christ. Amen.

SESSION 2: THE WITCH

Gathering

Open with prayer. Invite those gathered to go around the circle and share:
- —their names
- —a candy or junk food they might ask the White Witch for if they were in Edmund's place

Opening Discussion

Buy some Turkish Delight from a local Middle Eastern grocery to sample together. Try to buy as fresh and well-sealed a package (to avoid staleness) as possible. I recommend plain, hazelnut, or pistachio flavor. More expensive brands are generally of higher quality. You can also find it online and sometimes in big grocery stores with ethnic sections. Homemade by a local store is best. I've had success with Ogas, Koska, and Tunas brands. Hazer Baba is most common, but it is not the best tasting, in my opinion.

What do you think of Turkish Delight?

Why might C. S. Lewis have chosen Turkish Delight as the candy Edmund asks for?

powdery white like snow, sticky (like the situation Edmund is about to get himself into), foreign-sounding, which might have sounded sinister to a mid-century reader...

Entering the Story

Reading Aloud

Start at the end of chapter 3, with "The reindeer were about the size of Shetland ponies" and continue into chapter 4, ending with "He did not look either clever or handsome whatever the Queen might say." (If you choose and have time, read through to the end of chapter 4.)

You may want to ask participants to take turns reading by sentence or paragraph around the circle (inviting multiple readers is a good way to keep everyone engaged with what they're hearing). You can tell people they may "pass" if they would rather not read aloud.

Optional Movie Clip

Watch together the scene where Edmund walks through the wardrobe and meets the Witch. Stop when the Witch leaves in her sleigh. (Use any movie version.)

Reflection on the Story

Invite participants to share what they notice about the scene. Was there anything they were particularly drawn to? Anything they disliked? Compare the movie version to the book version of the scene, if you're using both.

What do you notice about Edmund?

often cruel and self-absorbed, doesn't like his siblings, has not brought a coat...

What do you think makes the White Witch so attractive to Edmund?

she's beautiful and powerful, seems to like and admire him, gives him a hot drink and Turkish Delight . . .

What clues could Edmund have seen that betray the Witch's sinister nature?

treats just disappear, they're magic and not real, the treats are addictive, she's cruel and indifferent to her servant . . .

How does the experience affect Edmund afterward?

cruel to his siblings, decides to plot against them and keep secrets, wants more Turkish Delight . . .

Deeper Discussion

1. Does the Witch remind you of a certain character in the Christmas story? Read Matthew 2:1–6 together, then compare and contrast King Herod and the Queen of Narnia. Why is the coming of Aslan and also of Christ so threatening to those in power?

2. Lewis, later in the book, calls the Turkish Delight of the Witch "bad magic food," as opposed to "good ordinary food" (see chap. 9). What "bad magic foods" are you craving this season, despite yourself? (May include activities or items that aren't literally foods.)

3. Much later in the story, Edmund repents and rejoins his siblings. If you have time, read the three paragraphs in chapter 13 where Edmund and Aslan have a conversation, and Edmund apologizes to his brother and sisters. How does this passage make you think about repentance?

4. Do you think of Advent as a season for repentance for yourself?

Closing Fun

Play the song "Turkish Delight" by the David Crowder Band, *Music Inspired by the Chronicles of Narnia*, available on CD or mp3.

Closing Prayer

God of Peace, as we walk further into the season of Advent, watching and waiting for your Son, journey with us. Help us to repent for what we have done or left undone. Give us courage to deepen our faith as we face the busy schedules and heightened expectations of the season. All this we ask in the name of Jesus Christ. Amen.

SESSION 3: FATHER CHRISTMAS

Gathering

Open with prayer. Invite those gathered to go around the circle and share:
- —their names
- —their memories of Santa Claus from when they were growing up

Opening Discussion

What words do you associate with Santa Claus? (Perhaps list these on a big piece of paper.)

Do you think of Santa Claus as a Christian figure in any way? Why or why not?

Entering the Story

Reading Aloud
Start in the middle of chapter 10, with "It seemed to Lucy only the next minute . . ." and read through the next few pages, ending with "the sledge and all were out of sight before anyone realized they had started."

You may want to ask participants to take turns reading

by sentence or paragraph around the circle (inviting multiple readers is a good way to keep everyone engaged with what they're hearing). You can tell people they may "pass" if they would rather not read aloud.

Optional Movie Clip
Watch together the scene where Father Christmas finds the Beavers and the children and then gives them their gifts. (Note that the animated version does not include Father Christmas.)

Reflection on the Story
Invite participants to share what they notice about the scene. Was there anything they were particularly drawn to? Anything they disliked? Compare the movie version to the book version of the scene, if you're using both.

How does Father Christmas prepare the way for Aslan?
showing Christmas has finally come, defeating winter, equipping the children and Narnians for battle, dispelling fear and bringing hope . . .

What are some similarities between Father Christmas and the commercial Santa Claus?
wear red, have white beards, drive sleighs pulled by reindeer, bring gifts, are strong and kind . . .

How is Father Christmas different?
more serious, brings "tools, not toys" and whole meals, brings gifts for animals, more connected to the salvation of Narnia whereas Santa Claus is separate from the story of the birth of Jesus . . .

What is the deeper meaning of the gifts to the children?
mirror their gifts as individuals, parallel to the Bible verse "the armor of God," tools of faith as well as for battle (see Eph. 6:10–17), gifts enable them to serve others . . .

Deeper Discussion

1. Have you ever considered that Father Christmas / Santa Claus and John the Baptist have some things in common? Read together Luke 3:7–18 and compare and contrast them.

    Similarities include: furry clothes, live on the outskirts of society in extreme climates, scary and intimidating, usually depicted with beards, notice bad behavior, encourage generosity . . .

2. What gift of Father Christmas to the children are you most drawn to? Why? How does that gift speak to your own spiritual journey, your talents, or your call from God to serve the world?

Closing Prayer

God of Joy, as we draw ever nearer to Christmas in this season of Advent, watching and waiting for your Son, journey with us. Help us prepare for his coming with solemnity and joy, taking seriously our own call to bring your gospel into the world. Give us courage to deepen our faith as we face the busy schedules and heightened expectations of the season. All this we ask in the name of Jesus Christ. Amen.

SESSION 4: THE LION

Gathering

Open with prayer. Invite those gathered to go around the circle and share:
- —their names
- —what they are most excited about or most anticipating about Christmas

Opening Discussion

Read aloud together some important biblical passages that mention lions: Revelation 5:5–6; Hosea 11:10; Isaiah 11:6–9.

How is Jesus like a lion, based on these passages? Do you recognize Aslan in these passages as well?

Entering the Story

Reading Aloud
Start near the beginning of chapter 7 with "A moment later the stranger came out from behind the tree . . ." and continue a few pages, ending with "the beginning of the holidays or the beginning of summer."

You may want to ask participants to take turns reading by sentence or paragraph around the circle (inviting multiple readers is a good way to keep everyone engaged with what they're hearing). You can tell people they may "pass" if they would rather not read aloud.

Optional Movie Clip
Watch together the scene where the children meet Mr. Beaver in the woods and he first mentions the name of Aslan to them. Stop before they reach the Beavers' house. (Use any movie version.)

Reflection on the Story
Invite participants to share what they notice about the scene. Was there anything they were particularly drawn to? Anything they disliked? Compare the movie version to the book version of the scene, if you're using both.

Review the different ways that each child reacts to the name of Aslan. What do you think you might feel? What do you notice about the reactions of the children, according to their personalities?

Have you ever felt similarly in response to the name or presence of God or Christ?

Deeper Discussion

1. In this novel, the savior is a lion, a creature that isn't human. This is fun for a children's story, but it also offers an image of Christ markedly different from the Gospels. What does meeting Christ in the form of a lion emphasize about his identity?
   power, strength, fierceness, otherness, his divinity rather than his humanity, connection to all creation and not just human beings . . .

2. Do you experience Aslan as a Christ figure? Is his spiritual leadership compelling for you? Why or why not?
3. What more tame and vulnerable creature do Christians often use to symbolize Jesus? (*A lamb.*) How is Jesus like a lamb? Are there ways Aslan is also like a lamb?
4. Invite the group to reflect on this quotation from Rowan Williams (taken from an interview published in *The Telegraph* newspaper in July 2012, after his book on the Narnia Chronicles, *The Lion's World*, was published): "There is a feeling [in Lewis's writing] that something really quite fierce has taken hold of people [when they turn to God]."

Closing Prayer

God of Love, as we draw near to Christmas, watching and waiting for your Son, journey with us. Grow in our hearts a sense of delight and holy fear at his coming, to change the world and redeem us from sin. Give us courage to deepen our faith as we face the busy schedules and heightened expectations of the season. All this we ask in the name of Jesus Christ. Amen.

CREATING A NARNIA NIGHT
FOR FAMILIES

Narnia Night can be a wonderful family event for your church. You can invite just children or both children and their parents. Narnia Night will be most fun for children between the ages of four and twelve. Teenagers can be invited to create decorations, staff activity stations, or even dress in costume. Let your Narnia Night reflect the interests and abilities of your church and volunteers—and have fun!

When you work hard on decorating for an event like this, it's no fun to take everything down after one night. Consider leaving "Narnia" intact for most of Advent, especially if you're also using the adult program in this book.

If your congregation *really* enjoys Narnia Night, consider continuing the theme into the summer with "Aslan Is on the Move," a well-done vacation Bible school program by Leader Resources (http://leaderresources.org/aslanisonthemove).

Decorations

Choose an area of your church to be "Narnia." You can transform several rooms or just a single doorway, depending on how much time and talent is available to you. Here are some ideas to help you get started, but be sure to explore online sites, such as Pinterest, or use a search engine to see what other churches or families have tried more recently.

Note: You don't have to create *all* of these to make for a magical evening. Choose what seems most doable for your context and volunteer team:

1. *Wardrobe:* Transform the doorway to your "Narnia" area with wardrobe doors made of cardboard, plywood, old closet doors, or cheap new ones from your local home improvement store, depending on your budget.
2. *Lamppost:* Use PVC pipe or cardboard tubes, painted black, and a yellow paper "flame" or a battery-powered tea light or lantern. You can also paint one on a large piece of butcher paper. Some party stores sell a large wall decal of a lamppost.
3. *Fur Coats:* Big wool coats can serve just as well; church members and thrift shops are good sources.
4. *Snow:* Use cotton batting or old white sheets.
5. *Forest:* Borrow a few artificial Christmas trees (without decoration) or a painted butcher paper background attached to a wall; or, you may be able to find a vendor selling real trees to reduce the price or even donate a few trees for a church program.
6. *Robin:* A toy robin or Christmas ornament, perched in one of the trees, will remind the children of the Robin in chapter 6.
7. *Mountains:* Consider including a painted paper background that shows the "two little hills" opposite the lantern, which shows the way to the Witch's castle (see chapter 4).
8. *Beaver's Home:* Use a child-sized or regular table, tablecloth, dishes, teapot, and cloth napkins; optional— boots, rocking chair, fishing gear, snowshoes, rug, etc.

9. *Witch's Sleigh*: Trick out a large cardboard box using a large folding table as a frame (in which case, no person should actually sit in/on it). You can also cheat a bit and set the sleigh/box right on the floor and not worry too much about depicting runners. You might harness up a reindeer from someone's lawn decoration collection, or find a stuffed reindeer or horse (just add antlers) of any size. It's not an essential detail, but in the novel, the Witch's reindeer are white rather than brown. Consider adding jingle bells, which are a prominent sound effect of the White Witch.

Activities

Help children and families get acquainted with the story, if they're not already, and make some connections between Narnia and Advent. Choose all or several of these ways to set the scene for your Narnia Night.

Kids and families can do the activities all together, one after the other, or as "stations" for them to visit in their own time. Choose the activities that best suit your congregation, probably no more than four.

Walk through the Wardrobe
Make walking through the wardrobe door a special part of the evening. If your wardrobe is near the church entrance or the entrance to the room or wing where Narnia Night will be held, families can pass through the door as they arrive and be "in Narnia" all evening. If there is a gathering area before families get to the wardrobe, consider introducing the night's activities before inviting them to walk through the wardrobe.

Tea with Mr. Tumnus

Serve everyone tea or cocoa with cookies as they arrive in Narnia, greet everyone, and allow some grace and space for latecomers. This can include:

— Music from the movie playing in the background
— Someone dressed as Mr. Tumnus walking around with an umbrella and asking if the children are "Daughters of Eve" and "Sons of Adam"
— Mr. Tumnus or another volunteer passing out name tags for children and adults

Watch a Movie

You can watch all or part of a movie version together; however, since families can easily do this at home, it might be more fun to be active together for your Narnia Night. (See appendix A for copyright warning and more information about the three most commonly available movie versions.)

Read Aloud

Have the children sit down and listen to someone (such as the Professor or Father Christmas) read to them from the book. The reader could explain to the children that this is a story about Jesus, as if Jesus had come to another world instead of ours (something Lewis said) or that the story is about a group of children meeting a Lion who reminds us of God or Jesus. Adapt the message to suit the kids' ages and maturity.

Read aloud the first chapter of the novel or purchase or borrow from your library the shortened, illustrated children's version of the novel available from author Hiawyn Oram (ISBN: 978-0060556501). Read the whole story or stop when the children meet Aslan, for the sake of time or if you think the violence later in the story would be too much for your church's kids.

Talk about Narnia and Advent
Create some dialogue about the story in the novel and the Christian story. Explain that this is one of many special stories a man named C. S. Lewis wrote about people and about God. Some older kids may have read some or all of them; invite them to raise their hands (they will love this). Their enthusiasm will get other kids excited about reading for themselves.

Use newsprint or a computer projector to write down and display the kids' answers. Make this shorter or longer depending on your kids' age span.

Advent and Narnia
—I wonder how Advent and Narnia are the same? Suggest that they look around at the decorations or remember the story or movie scenes.

The Pevensie Children and Baby Jesus
—I wonder how children see the world differently than grown-ups?
—I wonder why God sent Jesus as a little baby?

Aslan and Jesus
—I wonder how Jesus is like a lion?
—I wonder how Jesus is like Aslan?
—I wonder how Jesus is like a human?

Christmas and Springtime
—I wonder if there are ways that Christmas is like springtime?

Make an Aslan Ornament or Puppet

Have the children make the face of Aslan to hang on their Christmas trees and carry in the closing worship procession. Adapt details as needed.

Supplies
— Small paper plates
— Circles of yellow, orange, or brown felt, precut to fit the plate center (excluding rim)
— Plastic eyes or brown or black buttons for eyes
— Markers, crayons, or colored pencils
— Glue
— Scissors
— Tongue depressors OR hole punch and yarn
— 1–2 premade examples for parents and kids to work from

Instructions
1. Glue eyes (or buttons) to the felt circle (if using).
2. With a marker, draw a mouth and nose (and eyes, if needed).
3. Color the rim as the mane in orange, brown, black, or yellow.
4. Snip the rim with scissors at ½-inch intervals to "fluff" the mane.
5. Glue the felt circle to the center of the plate.
6. Glue a tongue depressor to the back to hold it as a puppet or punch a hole in the top and thread yarn to hang as an ornament.
7. Consider having a place for the kids to store their ornaments or puppets while they do other activities.

The White Witch's Winter Spell

The children add white or gray paper links to a chain symbolizing the power of the White Witch to keep Christmas from coming. Each child receives a few strips of paper to decorate with images of winter before linking them together.

Supplies
— White and gray construction paper, precut into long strips
— Black pens, markers, or pencils
— Glue, tape, or rubber cement to link the chains together

Instructions
1. Start with a chain of about ten links, decorated with snowflakes, bare trees, frowny faces, and words such as "winter," "sad," or "cold."
2. Have each child decorate three to five paper links, depending on age or interest, to show winter or the creatures of Narnia waiting for Aslan. Older children may want to write a word or sentence on their links.
3. Help the kids add their links to the chain with glue or tape.
4. Eventually, hang the chain in a prominent place and have the kids symbolically break it to show that the Witch's power is broken by Aslan. If you do a closing prayer time, you have the option of breaking the chain then.

Make a Lamppost
Older children can craft this paper lantern, reminiscent of the lamppost in the woods.

Supplies
— Black (or colored) construction paper or cardstock

- Cardstock rectangles for tracing the window panes of the lantern
- Pencils for tracing
- Scissors
- White tissue paper, precut into rectangles slightly larger than the tracers
- Glue or tape
- Stapler
- Yarn or string and hole punch OR paper towel tubes
- One or two premade examples for parents and kids to work from

Instructions
1. Trace four rectangles on the black paper in pencil to make window panes, i.e., with a cross at the center.
2. Cut out the panes.
3. Glue (or tape) tissue paper behind the windows panes.
4. Roll the paper into a tall cylinder and staple together.
5. Make two holes across from one another at the top and thread yarn or string for hanging.
6. Or, glue or staple a paper towel tube inside the lantern to make a lamppost (the kids could paint or staple black construction paper around the tube, too).
7. Consider having a place for the kids to store their lampposts while they do other activities. If you're using glue, it will need time to dry.

Try Some Turkish Delight
Consider placing this station near the Witch's sleigh, if that will be part of your decorating scheme.

Supplies
- Small table with a white (perhaps sparkly) cloth
- A fancy plate or box for the candy

—A box or two of Turkish Delight in plain, pistachio, or hazelnut flavor (rose flavor tends not to appeal to Western tastes). You can find it at Middle Eastern stores, online, and sometimes in big grocery stores. Homemade by a local store is great! I've had success with these brands: Ogas, Koska, Tunas. Hazer Baba is the most common, but it's not great tasting. More expensive brands are generally better quality. You can try to make a batch yourself, but this requires a candy thermometer, over an hour of simmering and stirring, and a cooling time of five hours. Many recipes are online.

—List of ingredients close at hand in case of allergies

—Paper napkins, because Turkish Delight is dusted with confectioners' sugar

—Optional: small cups of hot cocoa to represent the sweet, steaming drink the Witch gave to Edmund. This is also a good palette cleanser for those who won't like the candy.

—Trash can for waste or unfinished candy

Instructions

1. Set the candy out in a beautiful way for children and grown-ups to sample.
2. Have a costumed White Witch to serve it.

Make Fire-Flower Cordial

This is the cordial Lucy received from Father Christmas for healing. This activity would more accurately be called "bottling," since you make the cordial in advance.

Supplies
—Dixie cups
—Small, plastic cylindrical bottles with flip-top spouts

(there are lots of options for online purchase or you
might try a local drugstore or beauty supply shop)
— Small funnels
— Small pitchers, glass measuring cups, or anything
with a small spout
— Cran-raspberry juice or cranberry cocktail, mixed
with a little ginger ale or lemon lime soda. Store in a
tall pitcher with a lid.
— Labels that read "Fire-Flower Cordial" for kids to
decorate and attach to their bottles
— Note for parents: list of ingredients, with note to
refrigerate and consume within a week
— Cloth or paper towels to catch spills

Instructions
1. Color and decorate a label.
2. Attach label to a bottle.
3. Use a mini pitcher and funnel to fill the bottle with
red juice.
4. Cap the bottle and dry any drips.
5. Sample the cordial!
6. Consider having a place for the kids to store their
cordials while they do other activities.

Battle the Witch's Power — Whack a Winter Piñata!
Destroying the Witch's power is a true battle for the children and creatures of Narnia. As the Witch's power fades,
Christmas comes to Narnia! The children can take turns
hitting the piñata until Christmas candies or tokens fall
out. Find a piñata shape that embodies winter or the Witch
(a castle, a snowflake, a star). Be careful not to choose
something you will feel uneasy encouraging children to hit
and destroy.

Supplies
— Piñata, not the pull-string kind
— Christmas-themed candy and tiny toys for filling
— Piece of rope (not string, yarn, or twine) for hanging
— Blindfold: bandana, wide cloth strip
— A piñata stick, a baseball bat (plastic or wood), or broom handle
— Extra candy and toys to throw out to make sure all kids get some

Instructions
1. Fill the piñata well in advance in case you have technical difficulties.
2. Hang the piñata one to two feet above child eye level. Use a secure hook in the ceiling or secure on a clothesline strung between two very sturdy objects, hooks, or trees (weather permitting, this could be done outdoors). Do not have a human being hold the piñata.
3. Create a "safety zone" around the piñata that is guarded by an adult. Only the child with the stick can be in the safety zone.
4. Let the smallest children go first.
5. Allow each child to have three tries.
6. When the piñata breaks (an adult can help if this becomes problematic), have extra candy to throw on the ground to be sure all children get a share.

A Feast with the Beavers
Have dinner together as though you are dining with the Beavers (including a costumed Mr. and Mrs. Beaver is optional).

Supplies
— Plates, napkins, silverware, cups, etc.
— Centerpieces, perhaps woodland animals, teapots, mittens, boots, etc.
— Food (see menu ideas, below)

Menu
Find your own particular balance between authenticity and kid tastes. Before the meal begins, remind the kids that fish and bread are ancient Christian symbols and ask if they know what they stand for (*Eucharist, Communion, multiplying of the loaves and fishes, the "sign of the fish" that stands for the name of Jesus*). Ask one of the Beavers to welcome everyone or say grace, if present.

What the Beavers serve in the book:
— Milk
— Bread and butter
— Fried trout
— Boiled potatoes
— Mrs. Beaver's Sticky Marmalade Roll
— Hot tea
— Beer (only for Mr. Beaver.)

A kid-friendly middle ground:
— Fish sticks or chicken fingers
— Mashed potatoes or French fries
— Cocoa
— An Easy Recipe for Mrs. Beaver's Sticky Marmalade Roll (see appendix B)

A Visit from Father Christmas
Have Father Christmas come for a visit with a sack or sleigh of small gifts. In the novel, he looks like a modern

Santa: white beard and a red costume with white trim. He is more serious and thoughtful than a mall Santa, however.

Gifts he could bring, depending on your budget and age groups:

— Small toy lions
— Noisemakers (like Susan's horn)
— Plastic swords and shields
— Christmas ornaments: Mary and child, baby Jesus, lion
— Advent calendars
— Copies of the novel

Closing Prayer Service

Adapt for your congregation's worship style, or ask your pastor or priest to do so.

Procession
Process together around "Narnia" and then into your sanctuary. At the head of your procession, you might have, depending on your worship style:

— Your pastor/s
— A tall stick festooned with streamers
— A lion on the end of a stick or pole
— A processional cross

The children might carry noisemakers, the Aslan ornaments or lanterns (made during activity time), or their gifts from Father Christmas.

Song
As you process in or when you're gathered in the worship space:

— "O Come, O Come Immanuel"
— "This Little Light of Mine"

Opening Prayer
Leader: Light and Peace, in Jesus Christ our Lord.
People: Thanks be to God.
Leader: Jesus said, "I am the light of the world. Whoever
     follows me will never walk in darkness but will
     have the light of life" (John 8:12)

Reflection and Thank You
Leader gives a brief message about the meaning of the
evening, Narnia, and the meaning of Advent. The leader
thanks everyone for coming and the Narnia Night team for
their hard work.

Reading: Isaiah 11:6–9
Ask a child to read, if possible. (This is the Common English Bible translation)
> The wolf will live with the lamb,
>> and the leopard will lie down with the young goat;
>> the calf and the young lion will feed together,
>> and a little child will lead them.
> The cow and the bear will graze.
> Their young will lie down together,
>> and a lion will eat straw like an ox.
> A nursing child will play over the snake's hole;
>> toddlers will reach right over the serpent's den.
>>> They won't harm or destroy anywhere on my
>>> holy mountain.
>> The earth will surely be filled with the knowledge of
>> the LORD,
>> just as the water covers the sea.

The Lighting of the Advent Wreath

Breaking of the Witch's Chain of Winter
Leader gets the children to tell about the chain and about

the Witch's power to keep Christmas from coming. Since "Aslan is on the move" and the Advent Wreath has been lit, the Witch's power can be destroyed! Leader, perhaps with a few of the children, breaks apart the chain by hand or with scissors and scatters the pieces.

Closing Prayer
Leader: You are the light of the world.
People: Jesus is the light of all people.

Leader: The light shines in the darkness, and the darkness did not overcome it.
People: Come quickly, Lord Jesus.

Leader: Let us go in peace.
People: Thanks be to God.

APPENDIX A

Movie Versions of *The Lion, the Witch, and the Wardrobe*

Disney
(live action, 2005) 2 hours, 23 minutes: visually beautiful with excellent special effects; not altogether faithful to the book. This will be the version with which most people are familiar.

BBC (British Broadcasting Corporation)
(live action, 1988) 2 hours, 51 minutes: originally broadcast on television as the first of a three-part series, faithful to the book but with dated special effects, including giant puppets as the Beavers and Aslan. This version has a more measured pace and is less violent than the Disney version.

Children's Television Workshop
(animated, 1979) 1 hour, 35 minutes: shortest version, very charming, most closely follows the book, although the animation will seem dated. Father Christmas does not appear; the gifts are given to the children by Aslan.

Copyright Warning: You may show a movie in your church without permission as long as it is not advertised to the public; this is considered a face-to-face teaching activity. However, you must be using a legitimate, purchased copy of the movie (17 U.S.C. § 110(1)).

APPENDIX B

An Easy Recipe for Mrs. Beaver's Sticky Marmalade Roll

Mrs. Beaver's sticky marmalade roll would have been more like a jelly roll, but this is simpler and a crowd-pleaser.

This recipe gives ten people a taste or eight people a nice-sized portion.

The Roll
  1 tube refrigerated crescent dough
  2 Tbs. butter, melted
  3/4 cup orange marmalade
  ½ tsp. salt
  1 Tbs. brown sugar

The Sticky Glaze
  1 cup powdered sugar
  2 Tbs. butter, melted
  2 Tbs. orange juice
  2 Tbs. milk (or use all juice)
  dash salt

Instructions

1. Heat oven to 375°F. Grease 9-inch pie plate or 8- or 9-inch square glass baking dish with butter or cooking spray; set aside.
2. Unroll dough onto work surface. You will use it all in one piece, so press the seams closed with your fingers. To further seal and flatten, roll a few times with a rolling pin (optional).
3. Pour melted butter over dough and spread with a pastry brush or spoon. Top with marmalade, spreading evenly. Sprinkle with salt and sugar. Roll up dough, long side first. Pinch edge to seal. Cut into eight to ten slices. Set slices, spiral side up, in pie plate.
4. Bake for 20 minutes or until light golden brown.
5. Meanwhile, in small bowl, mix glaze ingredients until smooth. Drizzle over rolls either fresh out of the oven or after they cool. If you wait for them to cool, the glaze will stay on top of the rolls; if you drizzle when warm, the glaze will soak through them. Either is delicious.
6. Eat while still warm or at room temperature. You can also make them a day ahead and store them in an airtight container.

NOTES

1. Alan Jacobs, *The Narnian: The Life and Imagination of C. S. Lewis* (New York: Harper One, 2008), 243.
2. C. S. Lewis, "On Three Ways of Writing for Children," in *On Stories: And Other Essays on Literature* (San Diego: Harcourt Inc., 2002), 34.
3. Rowan Williams, *The Lion's World* (New York: Oxford University Press, 2012), 144.
4. Anne Lamott, *Bird by Bird: Some Instructions on Writing and Life* (New York: Knopf Doubleday, 2007), 236.
5. Williams, *The Lion's World*, 28.
6. Lewis, *On Stories*, 34.
7. C. S. Lewis, *Mere Christianity* (New York: Harper One, 1980), 77.
8. Williams, *The Lion's World*, 142.
9. C. S. Lewis, *Letters to Malcolm: Chiefly on Prayer* (New York: Harcourt, Brace, and World, 1964), 104.
10. James Baldwin, *Notes of a Native Son* (Boston: Beacon Press, 1983), 101.
11. Lewis, *Mere Christianity*, 205.